John Bunyan

The Child's Pilgrim's Progress

Vol. 1

John Bunyan

The Child's Pilgrim's Progress
Vol. 1

ISBN/EAN: 9783337292539

Printed in Europe, USA, Canada, Australia, Japan

Cover: Foto ©Lupo / pixelio.de

More available books at **www.hansebooks.com**

THE
CHILD'S
PILGRIM'S PROGRESS.

PART FIRST.

"I have used similitudes."
               Hosea xii. 10.

PHILADELPHIA:
PRESBYTERIAN BOARD OF PUBLICATION,
No. 821 Chestnut Street.

Entered according to Act of Congress, in the
year 1860, by
JAMES DUNLAP, Treas.,
in the Clerk's Office of the District Court of the
Eastern District of Pennsylvania.

S. D. WYETH, Stereotyper.

PREFACE.

No endeavour has been made in this little book to improve Bunyan's Pilgrim's Progress. To do so would be simply absurd.

To bring prominently into view scenes supposed most attractive to children has been attempted; and, while the Dreamer's narrative is preserved, others of less striking character have been thrown into the back ground.

The quaint, simple language of the incomparable Bunyan is, for the most part, retained.

CHILD'S PILGRIM'S PROGRESS.

As I walked through the wilderness of this world, I came to a certain place, and laid me down to sleep; and as I slept, I dreamed a dream.

I dreamed I saw a man clothed with rags, standing with his face from his own house, a book in his hand, and a great burden upon his back. I saw him open the book and read therein; and as he read he wept and trembled; and soon after, he brake out with a bitter cry, saying,

"What shall I do!"

Then, in great trouble, he went home, and tried, as long as he could, not to let his wife and children see his distress; but he could not be silent long. At length he spake his mind to them, and said, weeping,

"My dear wife and children, I find I am in myself undone by reason of a burden that lieth hard upon me. Moreover, I am certainly told that this our city will be burnt with fire; and that we all shall come to ruin, unless some way of escape can be found; which yet I see not."

At this his relatives were amazed; not that they believed what he said was true, but they thought some crazy fancy had got into his head. It being near night, they with all haste got him to bed, hoping that sleep would chase away his fears. But the night was as troublesome to him as the day; instead of sleeping, he spent it in sighs and tears.

So when the morning was come, they would know how he did. He told them, "Worse and worse."

He also set to talking to them again; but they would not hear him. Sometimes they would deride, sometimes they would chide, and sometimes they would quite neglect him. Wherefore he began to retire himself to his chamber, to pray for and pity them, and also to bewail his own misery.

He would also walk by himself in the fields, sometimes reading, and sometimes praying: and thus for some days he spent his time.

Now I saw, upon a time, when he was walking in the fields, that he was, as he was wont, reading in his Book, and greatly distressed in his mind; and as he read, he burst out, as he had done before, crying, "What shall I do to be saved?"

I saw also that he looked this way, and that way, as if he would run; yet he stood still, because he could not tell which way to go. I looked then, and saw a man named Evangelist, coming to him, and he asked,

"Wherefore dost thou cry?"
He answered,
"Sir, I see by the Book in my hand that I must die, and after that come to judgment."
Then said Evangelist,
"Why not willing to die, since this life is attended with so many evils?"
The man answered,
"Because I fear that this burden that is upon my back will sink me lower than the grave, and I shall fall into Tophet. I am not fit to go to judgment. The thoughts of these things make me cry."
Then said Evangelist,
"If this be thy condition, why standest thou still?"
He answered,

"Because I know not whither to go."

Then he gave him a parchment roll; and there was written within, 'FLEE FROM THE WRATH TO COME."

The man therefore read it, and looking upon Evangelist very carefully, said,

"Whither must I flee?"

Then said Evangelist, pointing with his finger over a very wide field,

"Do you see yonder wicket-gate?"

The man said,

"No."

Then said the other,

"Do you see yonder shining light?"

He said,

"I think I do."

Then said Evangelist, "Keep that light in your eye, and go up directly thereto, so shalt thou see the gate; at which, when thou knockest, it shall be told thee what thou shalt do."

So I saw in my dream that the man began to run. Now he had not run far, when his wife and children seeing it, began to cry after him to return; but the man put his fingers in his ears, and ran on, crying,

"Life! life! eternal life!"

The neighbours also came out to see him: and, some mocked, others threatened, and some cried after him to return; and among those that did so, were two resolved to fetch him back by force. The name of the one was Obstinate, and the name of the other Pliable. In a little time they overtook him.

Then said the man, to them, "Neighbours, wherefore are you come?"

They said,

"To get you to go back with us."

Thereupon they fell into an argument:—at length Christian, for that was the name of the man, persuaded Pliable to go with him; and Obstinate, quite angry, returned to his home in the city of Destruction, from whence they all had come.

Now I saw in my dream that

Slough of Despond.

when Obstinate was gone back, Christian and Pliable went along, talking, over the plain: and their talk was of heavenly things.

Now they drew nigh to a very miry slough that was in the midst of the plain; and they being heedless did both fall suddenly into the bog. The name of the slough was Despond. Here they wallowed for a time, being grievously bedaubed with the dirt; and Christian, because of the burden that was on his back, began to sink in the mire.

Then said Pliable,

"Ah, neighbour Christian, where are you now?"

"Truly," said Christian, "I do not know."

At that Pliable began to be offended, and angrily said,

"Is this the happiness you have told me of all this while? If we have such ill speed at our first setting out, what may we expect between this and our journey's end? May I get out again with my life, you shall possess the brave country alone for me."

And with that he gave a desperate struggle or two, and got out of the mire on that side of the slough which was next to his own house: so away he went and Christian saw him no more.

Christian was left to tumble in the slough of Despond alone: but still he endeavoured to struggle to that side of the slough that was farthest from his own house and next to the Wicket-gate. This he did, but could not get out because of the burden that was upon his back. But I saw in my dream, that a man came to him whose name was Help, and asked him,

"What dost thou here?"

"Sir," said Christian, "I was bid to go this way by a man called Evangelist, who directed me also to yonder gate, that I might escape the wrath to come. And as I was going thither, I fell in here."

"But why did you not look for the steps?" asked Help.

Christian answered: — "Fear followed me so hard, that I fled the next way, and fell in."

Then said he, "Give me thy

hand." And he drew him out, and set him upon sound ground, and bid him go on his way.

Now as Christian was walking along by himself, he espied one afar off, come crossing over the field to meet him. And they met just as they were crossing the way of each other. The gentleman's name that met him was Mr. Worldly Wiseman: he dwelt in the town of Carnal Policy, a very great town, and hard-by from whence Christain came. Mr. Worldly Wiseman had some guess of Christian; for his setting forth from the city of Destruction was much noised abroad. Now, seeing his laborious going, and hearing his sighs and groans, and the

Christian and Worldly Wiseman.

like, he began to enter into some talk with him.

This Mr. Worldly Wiseman was a lover of the world, and no friend of the Prince of Pilgrims. He told Christian to go to the house of Mr. Legality, in the town of Morality, who would ease him of his burden. His words beguiled the poor man, so that he was brought to a stand, and at last he turned out of his way to go to Mr. Legality's house.

But behold, when he was got now hard by a hill that had to be passed, it seemed so high, and also that side of it that was next the way-side, did hang so much over, that Christian was afraid to venture further, lest the hill should fall on his head; wherefore there he stood still, and wist not what to do. Also his burden now seemed heavier to him than while he was in his way. There came also flashes of fire out of the hill, that made Christian afraid that he should be burnt: here, therefore, he did sweat and quake for fear.

And now he began to be sorry that he had taken Mr. Worldly Wiseman's counsel; and with that he saw Evangelist coming to meet him, at the sight also of whom he began to blush for shame. So Evangelist drew nearer and nearer; and coming' up to him, he looked upon him with a severe and dreadful countenance, and thus began to reason with Christian.

"What dost thou here, Christian?" said he,

At which words Christian knew not what to answer; wherefore at present he stood speechless before him. Then said Evangelist further,

"Art not thou the man that I found crying without the walls of the city of Destruction?"

"Yes, dear sir, I am the man."

"Did not I direct thee the way to the little wicket-gate?"

"Yes, dear sir," said Christian.

"How is it then that thou art so quickly turned aside? For thou art now out of the way."

Then Christian told Evangelist all. How that he had met with Mr. Worldly Wiseman, and what he advised him to do. Evangelist reproved him from God's word, and showed him what dreadful hazard he had run.

Then Christian fell down at his feet as dead, crying, "Woe is me, for I am undone!"

At this sight Evangelist caught him by the right hand, saying, "All manner of sin and blasphemies shall be forgiven unto men." "Be not faithless, but believing."

Then did Christian again a little revive, and stood up trembling, as at first, before Evangelist.

Then Evangelist proceeded to show him wherein he had done wrong; and, as he went on, Christian's heart sank within him and he began to look for nothing but death, and cry out lamentably. At length he asked,

"Sir, what think you, is there any hope? May I now go back, and go up to the Wicket-gate? Shall I not be abandoned for this, and sent back from thence ashamed? I am sorry I have hearkened to this man's counsel: but may my sin be forgiven?"

Then said Evangelist to him, "Thy sin is very great, for by it thou hast committed two evils; thou hast forsaken the way that is good, to tread in forbidden paths. Yet will the man at the gate receive thee, for he has *goodwill* for men; only take heed that thou turn not aside again, 'Lest thou perish from the way, when his wrath is kindled but a little.'"

Then did Christian address himself to go back; and Evangelist after he had kissed him, gave him one smile and bid him, "God speed."

So he went on with haste, neither spake he to any man by the way.

So in process of time Christian got up to the gate. Now over the gate was written,

"Knock and it shall be opened unto you."

He knocked therefore, more than once or twice, saying,

"May I not enter here? Will he within
Open to sorry me, though I have been
An undeserving rebel? Then shall I
Not fail to sing his lasting praise on high."

PILGRIM'S PROGRESS. 29

Christian and Evangelist.

At last there came a grave person to the gate, named Good-will, who asked, Who is there? and Whence comest thou? and, What wouldst thou have?

Christian answered,

"Here is a poor burdened sinner. I come from the city of Destruction, but am going to Mount Zion, that I may be delivered from the wrath to come. Therefore, sir, since I am told that by this gate is the way thither, I would know if thou art willing to let me in?"

"I am willing with all my neart," said he; and with that he opened the gate.

So when Christian was stepping in, the other gave him a pull.

Then said Christian, "What means that?" The other told him, "A little distance from this gate there is erected a strong castle, of which Beelzebub is the captain; from thence both he, and they that are with him, shoot arrows at those that come up to this gate, if perhaps they may die before they can enter in."

Then said Christian, "I rejoice and tremble."

So when he got in the man at the gate asked him, Who directed thee hither? Christian answered, "Evangelist bid me come hither and knock, as I did; and he said, that thou, sir, wouldst tell me what I must do."

"An open door is set before thee and no man can shut it;" said Good-will.

Then Christian and Good-will fell into a long discourse, in which Christian told all that had happened to him since he left home; about Pliable and Obstinate, the Slough of Despond, his going out of the right way, of Mr. Worldly Wiseman and Evangelist. Good-will gave an attentive ear to him, and after reproving him, kindly gave him instruction on many points. At last he said,

"Come Christian, a little way with me, and I will teach thee about the way thou must go. Look before thee; dost thou see this narrow way? That is the way thou must go. It was cast up by the patriarchs, prophets, Christ, and his apostles, and it is as straight as a rule can make it: this is the way thou must go."

"But," said Christian, "are there no turnings nor windings, by which a stranger may lose his way?"

"Yes," answered Good-will, "there are many ways that branch off from this, and they are crooked and wide; but thus thou mayest distinguish the right from the wrong, the right only being straight and narrow."

Then Christian asked him, If he could not help him off with his burden that was upon his back?

But he told him,

"As to thy burden, be content to bear it, until thou comest to the place of deliverance; for there it will fall from thy back of itself."

Now Christian began to get ready to go upon his journey. So the other told him, that some distance from the gate, he would come to the house of the Interpreter, at whose door he should knock, and he would show him excellent things.

Then Christian took leave of his friend and he also bid him "God speed."

So he went on, till he came at the house of the Interpreter, where he knocked over and over, At last one came to the door, and asked,

"Who is there?"

"Sir," said Christian, "here is a traveller, who was bid to call here for profit; I would therefore speak with the master of the house."

So he called for the master of the house, who, after a little time, came to Christian, and asked him what he would have.

So Christian told him.

Then said the Interpreter,

"Come in; I will show thee that which will be profitable to thee."

So he commanded his man to light a candle, and bid Christian follow him to a private room, where he saw the picture of a very grave person hung up against the wall; and this was the fashion of it; it had eyes lifted up to heaven, the best of books in its hand, the law of truth was written upon its lips; the world was behind its back; it stood as if it pleaded with men, and a crown of gold did hang over its head.

Then Christian said, "What means this?"

"Now," said the Interpreter, "I have showed thee this picture first, because the man whose picture this is, is the only man whom the Lord of the place whither thou art going hath authorized to be thy guide in all difficult places: wherefore take good heed, lest in thy journey thou meet with some that pretend to lead thee right, but their way goes down to death."

Then he took him by the hand, and led into a very large parlor that was full of dust, because never swept; the Interpreter then called for a man to sweep. Now, when he began to sweep, the dust flew about so, that Christian was almost choked. Then said the Interpreter to a damsel that stood by, "Bring hither water, and sprinkle the room;" which, when she had done, it was swept and cleansed with pleasure.

Then said Christian, "What means this?"

The Interpreter answered, "This parlor is the heart of a man that was never sanctified by the gospel. The dust is his original sin, and inward corruptions.

He that began to sweep at first, is the law; but she that brought water, and did sprinkle it, is the gospel."

I saw moreover in my dream, that the Interpreter took him by the hand, and had him into a small room, where sat two little children, each one in his chair. The name of the eldest was *Passion*, and the name of the other *Patience*. Passion seemed to be much discontented, but Patience was very quiet.

Then Christian asked,

"What is the reason of the discontent of Passion?"

The Interpreter answered,

"The governor of them would have him stay for his best things till the beginning of the next year, but he will have all now; but Patience is willing to wait."

Then I saw that one came to Passion, with a bag of treasure, and poured it at his feet: the which he took up, and rejoiced therein, and withal laughed Patience to scorn. But I saw in a little while, he had lavished all away, and had nothing left him but rags.

Then I saw in my dream, that the Interpreter took Christian by the hand, and led him into a place where was a fire burning against a wall, and one standing by it, always casting much water upon it, to quench it; yet did the fire burn higher and hotter.

Then said Christian, "What means this?"

The Interpreter answered, "This fire is the work of grace that is wrought in the heart; he that casts water upon it, to put it out, is the devil: but in that thou seest the fire, notwithstanding, burn higher and hotter, thou shalt also see the reason of that."

So he had him about to the back side of the wall, where he saw a man with a vessel of oil in his hand, which he continually cast, but secretly, into the fire.

Then said Christian, "What means this?"

The Interpreter answered, "This is Christ, who continually, with the oil of his grace, maintains the work already begun in the heart."

I saw also, that the Interpreter took him again by the hand, and led him to a pleasant place, where was built a stately palace, beautiful to behold; at the sight of which Christian was greatly delighted. He saw also upon the top thereof certain persons walking, who were clothed all in gold.

Then said Christian, "May we go in thither?"

Then the Interpreter took him, and led him up towards the door of the palace; and behold, at the door stood a great company of men, desirous to go in, but durst not. There also sat a man at a little distance from the door, at a table-side, with a book and his inkhorn before him, to take the names of them that should enter therein ; he saw also that in the doorway stood many men in armour to keep it, being resolved to do to men that would enter, what hurt and mischief they could.

Now was Christian somewhat in amaze. At last, when every man started back for fear of the armed men, Christian saw a man of a very brave countenance come up to the man that sat there to write, saying,

"Set down my name, sir;" which when he had done, he saw the man draw his sword, and put a helmet on his head, and rush towards the door upon the armed men, who laid upon him with deadly force; but the man, not discouraged, fell to cutting and hacking most fiercely. So after he had received and given many wounds, he cut his way through, and pressed forward into the palace; at which there was a pleasant voice heard from those that were within, even of those that walked upon the top of the palace, saying,

"Come in, come in,
Eternal glory thou shalt win."

So he went in, and was clothed with such garments as they.

Then Christian smiled, and said,

"I think verily I know the meaning of this."

"Now," said Christian, "let me go hence."

"Nay, stay," said the Interpreter, "till I have showed thee a little more."

So he took him by the hand again, and led him into a very dark room, where there sat a man in an iron cage.

Now the man, to look on, seemed very sad; he sat with his eyes looking down to the ground, his hands folded together, and he sighed as if he would break his heart.

Then said Christian, "What means this?"

At which the Interpreter bid him talk with the man.

Then said Christian to the man, "What art thou?"

The man answered, "I was once a fair and flourishing professor, and had joy at the thoughts that I should get to the celestial city."

Chr. " Well, but what art thou now?"

Man. "I am a man of despair, and am shut up in it, as in this iron cage."

Chr. "But how camest thou into this condition?"

Man. "I left off to watch and be sober: I sinned against light, and the goodness of God; I have grieved the Spirit, and he is gone; I tempted the devil, and he is come to me; I have provoked

God to anger, and he has left me: I have so hardened my heart, that I cannot repent."

Then said Christian to the Interpreter,

"But is there no hope for such a man as this?"

"Ask him," said the Interpreter.

Then said Christian,

"Is there no hope, but you must be kept in the iron cage of despair?"

"No, none at all."

Chr. "Why, the Son of the Blessed is very pitiful."

Man. "I have crucified him afresh; I have despised his person, and his righteousness; I have counted his blood an unholy thing; I have done despite to the Spirit of grace, therefore I have shut myself out of all the promises, and there now remains to me nothing but threatenings, which shall devour me as an adversary."

Chr. "For what did you bring yourself into this condition?"

Man. "For the lusts, pleasures, and profits of this world; but now every one of those things bites me, and gnaws me like a burning worm."

Chr. "But canst thou not repent and turn?"

Man. "God hath denied me repentance; yea, himself hath shut me up in this iron cage: nor can all the men in the world let me out. Oh eternity, eternity! how shall I grapple with the misery that I must meet with in eternity?"

Then said the Interpreter to Christian,

"Let this man's misery be remembered by thee, and be an everlasting caution to thee."

"Well," said Christian, "this is fearful! God help me to watch and to be sober, and to pray that I may shun the cause of this man's misery. Sir, is it not time for me to go on my way now?"

Inter. "Tarry till I shall show thee one thing more, and then thou shalt go on thy way."

So he took Christian by the hand again, and led him into a chamber where there was one rising out of bed; and as he put on his raiment, he shook and trembled.

Then said Christian, "Why doth this man thus tremble?" The Interpreter then bid him tell to Christian the reason of his doing so.

So he began, and said,

"This night, as I was in my sleep, I dreamed, and behold the heavens grew exceeding black; also it thundered and lightened, that it put me into an agony. So I looked up in my dream, and saw the clouds rack at an unusual rate; upon which I heard a great sound of a trumpet, and saw also a man sitting upon a cloud, attended with the thousands of heaven: they were all in flaming fire; also the heavens were in a burning flame.

"I heard then a voice, saying, 'Arise, ye dead, and come to judgment.' And with that the rocks rent, the graves opened, and the dead that were therein came forth: some of them were exceeding glad, and looked upward; and some sought to hide themselves under the mountains.

"Then I saw the man that sat upon the cloud open the book, and bid the world draw near. I heard it also proclaimed to them that attended on the man that sat on the cloud, 'Gather together the tares, the chaff, and stubble, and cast them into the burning lake.' And with that the bottomless pit opened, just whereabout I stood; out of the mouth of which there came smoke, and coals of fire, with hideous noises. It was also said to the same persons, 'Gather my wheat into the garner.' And with that I saw many catched up and carried away into the clouds, but I was left behind. I also sought to hide myself, but I could not, for the man that sat upon the cloud still kept his eye upon me; my sins also came into my mind, and my conscience did accuse me on every side. Upon this I awoke from my sleep."

Chr. "But what was it that made you so afraid of this sight?"

Man. "Why, I thought that the day of judgment was come, and that I was not ready for it: but this frightened me most, that the angels left me behind. My conscience too afflicted me; and I thought, the Judge had always his eye upon me, showing indignation in his countenance."

Then said the Interpreter to Christian,

"Hast thou considered all these things!"

Chr. "Yes, and they put me in hope and fear."

Inter. "Well, keep all things so in thy mind, that they may be as a goad in thy sides, to urge thee forward in the way thou must go."

Now Christian began to get ready to go on his journey.

Then said the Interpreter, "The Comforter be always with thee, good Christian, to guide thee in the way that leads to the city."

So Christian went on his way, saying,

" Here I have seen things rare and profitable,
Things pleasant, dreadful, things to make me stable
In what I have begun to take in hand:
Then let me think on them, and understand
Wherefore they showed me were, and let me be
Thankful, O good Interpreter, to thee,"

Now I saw in my dream, that the highway up which Christian was to go, was fenced with a wall,

PILGRIM'S PROGRESS. 55

Christian loses his Burden.

called Salvation. Up this way, therefore, did burdened Christian run, but with difficulty, because of the load on his back.

He ran thus till he came at a place somewhat ascending; and upon that place stood a cross, and a little below, in the bottom, a sepulchre.

So I saw in my dream, that just as Christian came up with the cross, his burden loosed from off his shoulders, and fell from off his back, and began to tumble, and so continued to do, till it came to the mouth of the sepulchre, where it fell in, and I saw it no more.

Then was Christian glad and lightsome, and said with a merry heart,

"He hath given me rest by his sorrow, and life by his death."

Then he stood still awhile, to look and wonder; for it was very surprising to him that the sight of the cross should thus ease him of his burden. He looked, therefore, and looked again, even till the tears ran down his cheeks.

Now as he stood looking and weeping, behold, three Shining Ones came to him, and saluted him with, "Peace be to thee."

So the first said to him, "Thy sins be forgiven thee." The second stripped him of his rags, and clothed him with change of raiment. The third also set a mark on his forehead, and gave him a roll with a seal upon it, which he bid him look on as he ran, and that he should give it in at the celestial gate; so they went their way.

Then Christian gave three leaps for joy, and went on singing,

"Thus far did I come laden with my sin,
Nor could aught ease the grief that I was
 in,
Till I came hither. What a place is this!
Must here be the beginning of my bliss?
Must here the burden fall from off my
 back?
Must here the strings that bound it to me
 crack?
Blest cross! blest sepulchre! blest rather,
 be
The Man that there was put to shame for
 me!"

I saw then in my dream, that he went on thus even until he came at the bottom, where he saw, a little out of the way, three men fast asleep with fetters upon their heels. The name of one was Simple, of another Sloth, and of the third Presumption.

Christian seeing them lie went to awake them, and cried, You are like them that sleep on the top of a mast, for the Dead Sea is under you, a gulf that hath no bottom: awake, therefore, and come away. He also told them, If he that goeth about like a roaring lion, comes by, you will certainly become a prey to his teeth. With that they looked upon him, and began to reply in this sort:

Simple said, "I see no danger."

Sloth said, "Yet a little more sleep."

PILGRIM'S PROGRESS. 61

Simple, Sloth, and Presumption, asleep.

And Presumption said, "Every tub must stand upon its own bottom."

And so they lay down to sleep again, and Christian went on his way, feeling much troubled about them.

And as he went along he espied two men come tumbling over the wall, on the left hand of the narrow way; and they made up apace to him. The name of the one was Formalist, and the name of the other Hypocrisy. So they drew up to him, and entered into discourse.

They soon showed by their talk, as they had already done by their climbing over the wall instead of coming in at the Wicket-gate, that they were no true pilgrims.

They even laughed at what Christian told them of his experience; so he withdrew from them and walked on by himself. He would also often read in the roll that one of the Shining Ones gave him, by which he was greatly refreshed. I beheld then, that they all went on till they came to the foot of the hill Difficulty, at the bottom of which there was a spring. There were also at this place two other ways besides that which came straight from the gate: one turned to the left hand, and the other to the right; but the narrow way lay right up the hill Difficulty. Christian now went to the spring, and drank thereof to refresh himself, and then began to go up the hill, saying,

"The hill, though high I covet to ascend;
The difficulty will not me offend;
For I perceive the way to life lies here:
Come, pluck up heart, let's neither faint nor fear.
Better, though difficult, the right way to go,
Than wrong, though easy, where the end is woe."

The others also came to the foot of the hill, But when they saw that the hill was steep and high, and that there were two other ways to go; they resolved to go in those ways. Now the name of one of those ways was Danger, and of the other Destruction. So the one took the way called

Danger, which led him into a great wood; and the other took directly up the way to Destruction, which led him into a wide field, full of dark mountains, where he stumbled and fell, and rose no more.

I looked then after Christian, to see him go up the hill, where he went from running to walking, and from walking to clambering upon his hands and his knees, because of the steepness of the place.

Now about the midway to the top of the hill was a pleasant Arbour, made by the Lord of the hill for the refreshment of weary travellers. Thither, therefore, Christian got, where also he sat down to rest. Then he pulled his

Christian in the arbour.

roll out of his bosom, and read therein. He also now began afresh to take a review of the coat or garment that was given to him as he stood by the cross. Thus pleasing himself awhile, he at last fell into a slumber, and thence into a sound sleep, which detained him in that place until it was almost night; and in his sleep his roll fell out of his hand.

Now, as he was sleeping, there came one to him, and awaked him, saying, "Go to the ant, thou sluggard; consider her ways, and be wise." And with that Christian suddenly started up, and sped him on his way, and went apace till he came to the top of the hill.

Now when he was got up to the top of the hill, there came two men running amain; the name of the one was Timorous, and of the other Mistrust: to whom Christian said,

"Sirs, what's the matter? you run the wrong way."

They were in great terror and affright, and Mistrust said,

"A couple of lions lie in the way, whether sleeping or waking we know not; and we could not but think, if we came within reach, they would pull us in pieces."

Then was Christian afraid, but he resolved still to go forward. So Mistrust and Timorous ran down the hill, and Christian went on his way.

But thinking again of what he had heard from the men, he felt in his bosom for his roll, that he might read therein and be comforted; but he felt and found it not. Then was Christian in great distress, and knew not what to do. At last he bethought himself that he had slept in the arbour; and falling down upon his knees, he asked of God forgiveness for that foolish act, and then went back to look for his roll. As he went back, he kept carefully looking on this side and on that, all the way, if happily he might find it. He went thus till he came to the arbour where for a while he sat down and wept. At last, as Providence would have it, looking sorrowfully down under the settle there he espied his roll; with trembling haste he caught it up and put it into his bosom. But who can tell how joyful he was when he had gotten his roll again?

After he had given thanks to God for directing his eye to the place where it lay, with joy and tears he betook himself again to his journey. But O, how nimbly did he go up the rest of the hill! Yet before he got up, the sun went down upon Christian. Then he remembered what Mistrust and Timorous told him of the lions; and he said to himself, "These beasts range in the night; and if they should meet with me in the dark, how should I escape being torn in pieces!" Thus he went on his way.

But while he was bewailing his unhappy state he lifted up his eyes and behold there was a very stately palace before him, the name of which was Beautiful, and it stood by the highway-side.

So I saw in my dream that he made haste, that if possible he might get lodging there. Now before he had gone far, he entered into a very narrow passage, which was about a furlong off the porter's lodge; and looking very narrowly before him as he went, he espied two lions in the way.

The lions were chained, but he saw not the chains. Then he was afraid, and thought to go back.

But the porter at the lodge, whose name was Watchful, seeing that Christian made a halt, cried unto him saying "Fear not the lions, for they are chained; keep in the midst of the path, and no hurt shall come unto thee."

Then I saw that he went on, trembling but taking good heed to the directions of the porter; he heard them roar, but they did him no harm. Then he clapped his hands, and went on till he came to the gate. Then said Christian to the porter,

"Sir, what house is this? and may I lodge here to-night?"

The porter answered, "This house was built by the Lord of the hill, for pilgrims." The por-

Lions in the path.

ter also asked whence he was, and whither he was going.

After Christian had answered these and other questions, Watchful said he would call out one of the virgins of the place, who would according to their rules, if she liked his talk, admit him into the house. So he rang a bell, at the sound of which came out of the door a grave and beautiful damsel named Discretion, and asked why she was called.

Then Watchful told her of Christian's desire, whereupon she fell into discourse with him;— and shortly called out three more of the family, Prudence, Piety, and Charity, who after further talk with him, led him into the family and many of them meeting him at the threshold of the house, said,

"Come in thou blessed of the Lord; this house was built by the Lord of the hill on purpose to entertain such pilgrims in."

Then he bowed his head, and followed them into the house. So when he was come in and sat down, they gave him some refreshment, and consented together that, until supper was ready, some of them should have some particular discourse with Christian, for the best improvement of time ; and they appointed Piety, Prudence, and Charity to discourse with him.

So they continued talking

together of such things as are nearest to the hearts of pilgrims, until supper was ready; and Christian told them all that had happened to him on his way, and also of what he had learned since he started on pilgrimage.

Now I saw in my dream, that thus they sat talking together until supper time. So then they sat down to meat. Now the table was furnished with fat things, and with wine well refined; and all their talk at the table was about the Lord of the hill and his love to them; and by what they said, I perceived that he had been a great warrior, and had fought with and slain him that had the power of death; but not without great danger to himself, which made me love him the more.

Thus they discoursed together till late at night ; and after they had committed themselves to their Lord for protection, they retired to rest.

The pilgrim they laid in a large upper chamber, whose window opened towards the sun-rising. The name of the chamber was Peace, where he slept till break of day, and then he awoke and sang a hymn of thanksgiving.

So in the morning they told him that he should not depart till they had shown him the rarities of that place.

And first they led him into the study, where they showed him records of the greatest antiquity; they showed him the pedigree of the Lord of the hill, that he was the Son of the Ancient of days, and came by eternal generation. Here also were more fully recorded the acts that he had done, and the names of many hundreds that he had taken into his service.

Then they read to him also some of the worthy acts that some of his servants had done; and afterwards from another part of the records where it was shown how willing their Lord was to receive into his favour any, even any, though they in time past had offered great affronts to him.

The next day they took him, into the armoury, and showed him what their Lord had provided for pilgrims, as sword, shield, helmet, breastplate, and shoes that would not wear out.

Then I saw in my dream, that on the morrow they desired him to stay till the next day also ; and said " We will, if the day be clear, show you the Delectable Mountains ;"so he consented and stayed.

When the morning was up, they took him to the top of the house, and bade him look south. So he did, and behold, at a great distance. he saw a most pleasant mountainous country, beautified with woods, vineyards, fruits of all sorts, flowers also, with springs and fountains, very delectable to behold.

Then he asked the name of the country. They said, "It is Immanuel's land; and it is common to and for all pilgrims. And when thou comest there, from thence thou mayest see to the gate of the celestial city, as the shepherds that live there will make appear."

Now he bethought himself of setting forward. So they took him again into the armoury and harnessed him from head to foot with armour that was of proof.

He being therefore thus accoutred, walked out with his friends to the gate; and there he asked the porter if he saw any pilgrims pass by. Then the porter answered, Yes.

"Pray, did you know him?" said Christian.

"I asked his name, and he told me it was Faithful."

"O," said Christian, "I know him; he is my townsman, my near neighbour. How far do you think he may be before?"

Porter. "He is got by this time below the hill."

"Well," said Christian, "good porter, the Lord be with thee, and add to all thy blessings much increase for the kindness that thou hast showed me."

Then he began to go forward; but Discretion, Piety, Charity, and Prudence went with him down the hill.

Then said Christian, "As it was

difficult coming up, so, I see, it is dangerous going down."

"Yes," said Prudence, "it is a hard matter for a man to go down into the valley of Humiliation, and catch no slip by the way; therefore we are come out to accompany thee." So he began to go down, but very warily; yet he caught a slip or two.

Then I saw in my dream, that when Christian was got down to the bottom of the hill, they gave him a loaf of bread, a bottle of wine, and a cluster of raisins; and then he went on his way.

But now, in this valley of Humiliation, poor Christian was hard put to it; for he had gone but a little way before he espied a foul fiend coming over the field to meet him: his name was Apollyon.

Then did Christian begin to be afraid, and to cast in his mind whether to go back, or to stand his ground. But he considered again, that he had no armour for his back, therefore he resolved to venture and stand his ground.

So he went on, and Apollyon met him. Now the monster was hideous to behold: he was clothed with scales like a fish; he had wings like a dragon, and feet like a bear, and out of his belly came fire and smoke, and his mouth was as the mouth of a lion.

When he was come up to Christian, he beheld him with a

disdainful countenance, and began to question him.

"Whence came you, and whither are you bound?"

"I am come from the city of Destruction, which is the place of all evil, and I am going to the city of Zion," replied Christian.

Then Apollyon laid claim to him, and abused the Prince, under whom Christian served. He upbraided Pilgrim with all the mishaps of his journey, and told him he should proceed no farther, and broke out into a grievous rage.

So Apollyon straddled himself quite over the whole breadth of the way, and said to him,

"Prepare thyself to die; for I swear by my infernal den, that thou shalt go no farther: here will I spill thy soul."

And with that he threw a flaming dart at his breast; but Christian had a shield in his hand, with which he caught it, and so prevented the danger of that.

Then did Christian draw, for he saw it was time to bestir him; and Apollyon as fast made at him, throwing darts as thick as hail; so notwithstanding all Christian could do, Apollyon wounded him in his head, his hand, and foot. This made Christian give a little back: Apollyon, therefore, followed his work amain, and Christian again took courage, and resisted as manfully as he could.

This sore combat lasted for

above half a day, even till Christian was almost quite spent.

Then Apollyon, espying his opportunity, began to gather up close to Christian, and wrestling with him, gave him a dreadful fall; and with that Christian's sword flew out of his hand. Then said Apollyon, "I am sure of thee now:" and with that he had almost pressed him to death, so that Christian began to despair of life.

But, as God would have it, while Apollyon was fetching his last blow, Christian nimbly reached out his hand for his sword, and caught it, saying, "Rejoice not against me, O mine enemy: when I fall, I shall arise;" and with that he gave him a deadly thrust, which made him give back, as one that had received his mortal wound.

Christian perceiving that, made at him again, saying, "Nay, in all these things we are more than conquerors, through Him that loved us." And with that Apollyon spread forth his dragon wings, and sped him away, that Christian saw him no more.

In this combat no man can imagine, unless he had seen and heard, as I did, what yelling and hideous roaring Apollyon made; he spoke like a dragon: and on the other side, what sighs and groans burst from Christian's heart. It was the most dreadful sight that ever I saw.

So when the battle was over, Christian said, "I will here give thanks to Him that hath delivered me out of the mouth of the lion, to him that did help me against Apollyon." And so he did.

Then there came to him a hand with some of the leaves of the tree of life, which Christian took and applied to his wounds, and was immediately healed.

He also sat down in that place to eat bread, and to drink of the bottle that was given him a little before: so, being refreshed, he addressed himself to his journey with his sword drawn in his hand.

But he met with no other affront from Apollyon quite through this valley.

Now at the end of this valley was another, called the Valley of the Shadow of Death; and here Christian was worse put to it than in his fight with Apollyon.

For when Christian was got to the borders of the Shadow of Death, there met him two men, making haste to go back.

"Back! back!" they said, as they ran, "if either life or peace is prized by you."

But Christian knowing that his path was straight ahead, did not heed their words.

So they parted, and Christian went on his way, his sword still drawn in his hand.

PILGRIM'S PROGRESS. 93

Valley of the Shadow of Death.

I saw as far as this valley reached, there was on the right hand a very deep ditch; and again, on the left hand there was a very dangerous quag.

The pathway was here also exceeding narrow, so Christian, when he sought, in the dark, to shun the ditch, was ready to tip over into the mire; also, when he sought to escape the mire, he would be ready to fall into the ditch.

Thus he went on, and I heard him here sigh bitterly; for when he lifted up his foot to go forward, he knew not where or upon what he should set it next.

About the midst of this valley I perceived the mouth of hell to be, and it stood also hard by the wayside. Now, thought Christian, what shall I do? And ever and anon the flame and smoke would come out, with sparks and hideous noises—things that cared not for Christian's sword, as did Apollyon before — that he was forced to put up his sword, and betake himself to another weapon, called All-prayer: so he cried, in my hearing, "O Lord, I beseech thee, deliver my soul."

Thus he went on a great while. Sometimes he had half a thought to go back; then again he thought he might be half-way through the valley. So he resolved to go on; yet the fiends seemed to come nearer and nearer. But when they were come even almost at him, he cried out with a most vehement voice, "I will walk in the strength of the Lord God." So they gave back, and came no farther.

One thing I must mention. I took notice that now Christian was so confounded that he did not know his own voice, for when he was come near the mouth of the burning pit, one of the wicked ones got behind him, and whisperingly suggested many grievous blasphemies, which he verily thought had come from his own mind. This put Christian more to it than any thing before, even to think that he should now blaspheme Him that he had loved so much. Yet he had not the discretion either to stop his ears, or to know from whence these blasphemies came.

When Christian had travelled in this disconsolate condition some considerable time, he thought he heard the voice of a man, as going before him, saying, "Though I walk through the valley of the Shadow of Death, I will fear no evil, for thou art with me."

Then he was glad, for he hoped to have company by-and-by. So he went on, and called to him that was before; but he knew not what to answer, for that he also thought himself to be alone. And by-and-by the day broke: then said Christian, "He hath turned the shadow of death into the morning."

Now morning being come, he looked back to see, by the light of the day, what hazards he had gone through in the dark.

Now was Christian much affected with his deliverance from all the dangers he had passed. And about this time the sun was rising, and this was another mercy to Christian: for though the first part of the valley of the Shadow of Death was dangerous, yet this second part was, if possible, far more dangerous; for, from the place where he now stood, to the end of the valley, it was all along set so full of snares, traps, gins, and nets here, and so full of pits, pitfalls, deep holes, and shelvings-down there, that had it now been dark, had he had a thousand souls, they had in reason been cast away; but, as I said, just now the sun was rising. In this light, therefore, he came to the end of the valley.

Now I saw in my dream, that at the end of the valley lay blood, bones, ashes, and mangled bodies of men; and while I was musing what should be the reason, I espied a little before me a cave, where two cruel giants, Pope and Pagan, dwelt in old times. But by this place Christian went without much danger, because that Pagan had been dead many a day; and the other was grown so crazy and stiff in his joints that he can do little more than sit in his cave's mouth, grinning at pilgrims as they go by, and biting his nails because he cannot come at them.

So he spoke to him, though he could not go after him, saying, "You will never mend till more of you be burned." But he held his peace; and so went by, and catched no hurt. Then sung Christian, joyful, at all his deliverances.

Now, as Christian went on, he came to a little ascent; up which he went; and loking forward, he saw Faithful before him.

Then said Christian aloud,

"Ho, ho; so-ho; stay, and I will be your companion."

At that Faithful looked behind him; to whom Christian cried again,

"Stay, stay, till I come up to you."

But Faithful answered, "No, I am upon my life, and the avenger of blood is behind me."

At this Christian putting to all his strength, quickly got up with Faithful, and did also outrun him; so the last was first.

Then did Christian vain-gloriously smile, but not taking good heed to his feet, he stumbled and fell, and could not rise again until Faithful came up to help him.

PILGRIM'S PROGRESS. 103

Faithful and Christian.

Then I saw in my dream, they went very lovingly on together, and had sweet discourse of all things that had happened to them in their pilgrimage.

Faithful had been tried on his way with some temptations different from those that had assailed Christian. He did not fall into the slough of Despond, but he met with one whose name was Wanton;—from her however he was mercifully preserved.

Then, at the foot of the hill Difficulty there came up to him a very aged man, from the town of Deceit, who said his name was Adam the First, who offered him tempting wages to serve him. Faithful was sorely put to it, for he spoke very fair, but looking on his forehead as he talked with him he saw written there, "Put off the old man with his deeds." So he turned away from him, but the old man gave him when he left, such a deadly twitch back, that Faithful said, "I thought he had pulled part of me after himself."

When Faithful had gotten a good distance up the hill, about the place where the arbour was built, he saw one coming up very swiftly, after him. As soon as he got up to him he knocked him down for dead. When Faithful came to a little he asked him, wherefore he served him so. He said, because of his secret inclining to Adam the First. And so struck him again, and beat him. Faithful cried for mercy but he showed him none. But One came by that bade him forbear.

Christian asked, "Who was that who bade him forbear."

Faith. "I did not know him at first: but as he went by, I perceived the holes in his hands and in his side: then I concluded that he was our Lord. So I went up the hill."

Chr. That man that overtook you was Moses. He spareth none; neither knoweth he how to show mercy to those that transgress the law.

Then Faithful told Christian, that he had met in the valley of

Humiliation with one Discontent who strove hard, but by the grace of God in vain, to get him to go back. And also with another, a bold faced impudent fellow called Shame, who could scarcely be got rid of, and who caused him great trouble. After parting with these, he had sunshine the rest of the way, and also through the valley of the Shadow of Death.

Moreover I saw in my dream, that as they went on their way taking sweet counsel together, Faithful, as he chanced to look on one side, saw a man whose name was Talkative, walking a little off beside them; for in this place there was room enough for them all to walk. He was a tall man, and comely at a distance.

Faithful soon hailed the man who was as to appearance, a brave pilgrim and he was much taken with him. His tongue was ready to discourse on any subject, and he prated well about religion.

But Christian who had some knowledge of him, kept himself aloof, at which Faithful began to wonder.

Stepping up to Christian, Faithful asked him softly about their new companion. Then Christian told him what he knew of Talkative. That he was the son of one Say-well, and lived in Prating-Row in the town of Destruction, and that there was no true piety in him.

Faithful, thus put upon his guard, when he returned, spoke more warily, and bringing forward certain tests found that what Christian said was, alas, true. Talkative soon became offended at him, and of his own choice withdrew from his company.

Then up came Christian, and said to his brother,

"I told you how it would happen; your words and his lusts could not agree. He had rather leave your company than reform his life. But he is gone, as I said: let him go; the loss is no man's but his own. He has saved us the trouble of going from him; for he would have been but a blot in our company; besides,

PILGRIM'S PROGRESS. 111

In sight of Vanity-town.

the apostle says, 'From such withdraw thyself.'"

Faith. But I am glad we had this little discourse with him; it may happen that he will think of it again: however, I have dealt plainly with him, and so am clear of his blood if he perisheth."

Thus they went on, talking of what they had seen by the way, and so made that way easy which would otherwise no doubt have been tedious to them, for now they went through a wilderness.

Now when they were got almost out of this wilderness, Faithful cast his eye back, and espied Evangelist coming after them, at which they both were glad.

So after Evangelist had come

up and kindly saluted them, he enquired,

"How hath it fared with you my friends since our last parting?"

Then Christian and Faithful told him of all that had happened to them; and how and with what difficulty they had arrived to that place.

"Right glad am I," said Evangelist, "not that you have met with trials, but that you have been victors, and have notwithstanding many weaknesses, continued in the way to this very day."

He then spoke of other trials that awaited them; and told them that soon they would be sore put to it, in the town of Vanity which was just before them, and through which their pathway lay.

Then I saw that when they were come out of the wilderness, the town of Vanity lay before them; and at the town there is a fair kept all the year long, called Vanity Fair: a fair wherein all sorts of vanity are sold.

Now the pilgrims, must needs go through this fair. Well, behold, even as they entered into the fair, all the people were moved and the town itself was as it were in a hubbub about them.

The clothing and speech of the pilgrims were all unlike that of those who dealt at the fair: furthermore they set no value upon their wares. Those who traded there looked upon them with contempt, as though they were men not of sane mind, and scoffed and jeered at them.

One chanced, mockingly, to ask them, "What will ye buy?" But they looking gravely upon him, said, "We buy the truth." At last, things came to a great stir in the fair, so that all order was gone. Now was word brought to the great one of the fair, who quickly came down, and deputed some of his most trusty friends to take these men into examination.

So the men were brought before them, and being roughly questioned were afterwards beaten

Vanity Fair.

and then besmeared with dirt, and put into a cage, that they might be made a spectacle to all the men of the fair. There, therefore, they lay for some time, and were made the objects of sport, or malice, or revenge; the great one of the fair laughing still at all that befell them. But the men being patient, and giving good words for bad, and kindness for injuries, some in the fair that were less prejudiced, began to check and blame the baser sort for the abuses done to the men.

These angrily retorted;—and thus, after divers words had passed on both sides, they fell to some blows among themselves.

Then were these two poor men

brought before their examiners again, and were charged as being guilty of the new hubbub in the fair. So they beat them pitifully and hanged irons upon them, and led them in chains up and down the fair.

Now Christian and Faithful behaved themselves so wisely, and received the ignominy and shame that was cast upon them with so much meekness and patience, that it won to their side, several of the men in the fair, though but few in comparison of the rest. This put the other party into a greater rage, insomuch that they now determined upon their death.

Then were they put into the

cage again, and their feet made fast in the stocks.

A convenient time being appointed, they were brought forth to trial, in order to their condemnation. The judge's name was Lord Hate-good; their indictment was the same in substance, though somewhat varying in form; the contents whereof was this; "That they were enemies to, and disturbers of, the trade; that they had made commotions and divisions in the town, and had won a party to their own most dangerous opinions, in contempt of the law of their prince."

As might be supposed the judgment of this wicked court went against Faithful, whose life was the first that was sought; so a verdict was brought in against him, of guilty of death.

Therefore he was presently condemned to be led from the place where he was to the place from whence he came, and there to be put to the most cruel death that could be invented.

They then brought him out, to do with him according to their law; and first they scourged, then they buffeted him, then they lanced his flesh with knives; after that they stoned him with stones, then pricked him with their swords; and, last of all, they burned him to ashes at the stake. Thus came Faithful to his end.

Now I saw that there stood be-

Scoffing at Faithful and Christian.

hind the multitude a chariot and couple of horses waiting for Faithful, who so soon as his adversaries had dispatched him, was taken up into it, and straightway was carried up through the clouds with sound of trumpet, the nearest way to the Celestial gate.

But, as for Christian, he had some respite, and was remanded back to prison; so he there remained for a space. But he who overrules all things, having the power of their rage in his own hand, so brought it about that Christian for that time escaped them and went his way.

And as he went on his way he sang.

Now I saw in my dream, that Christian went not forth alone; for there was one whose name was Hopeful—being so made by the beholding of the behaviour of Christian and Faithful,—who joined himself unto him, and told him that he would be his companion. This Hopeful also told Christian that there were many more of the men in the fair that would take their time and follow after.

So I saw, that soon after they were got out of the fair, they overtook one that was going on briskly before them, whose name was By-ends; but with him they did not long keep company, for they found that he, like many others they had met with, was only a pilgrim in name. By-ends was one who did not stand up for Religion when in rags and contempt, but was zealous only when he walks in his silver slippers, in the sunshine, and with applause.

Now I saw in my dream, that after Christian and Hopeful forsook him, and kept their distance three men came up with him; their names were, Mr. Hold-the-world, Mr. Money-love and Mr. Save-all.

So after saluting each other in a friendly manner, these men fell into a discourse about Christian and Hopeful, wherein they came to the conclusion that they were most unwise and fanatical, and hastening after them, endeavoured to persuade them to adopt their principles of holding on to the world with one hand, while they grasped at heaven with the other. But in a few words, drawn from the Holy Writings, Christian put them to silence. So they stood staring one upon another, but had not wherewith to answer Christian. Hopeful also approved of Christian's answer; so there was a great silence among them.

Mr. By-ends and his company staggered and kept behind, so that Christian and Hopeful might outgo them. Then said Christian to his fellow, "If these men cannot stand before the sentence of men, what will they do with the sentence of God?"

Then Christian and Hopeful outwent them again, and went till they came to a delightful plain, called Ease, where they went with much content; but that plain was but narrow, so they quickly got over it.

Now at the farther side of that plain was a little hill, called Lucre, and in that hill a silver mine, which some that had formerly gone that way, had turned aside to see ; but going too near the brim of the pit, the ground, being deceitful under them, broke, and they were slain : some also had been maimed there, and were not restored again to their dying day.

Then I saw in my dream that

a little off the road, over against the silver mine, stood Demas, gentleman-like, to call passengers to come and see.

He called out to Christian and his fellow ; now Hopeful was disposed to go but Christian held him back—so they passed on their way.

By this time By-ends and his companions were come again within sight, and at the first beck went over to Demas. Now, whether they fell into the pit, or whether they went down to dig, or whether they were smothered by the damps that commouly rise from these things, I am not certain ; but this I observed, that they were never again seen in the way.

Now I saw that just on the other side of this plain the pilgrims came to an old monument. The form was as if it had been a woman transformed into the shape of a pillar. Upon it they looked and looked, a long while. At last Hopeful espied, written upon the head thereof, a writing; but he being no scholar, called to Christian, to see if he could pick out the meaning: so, after a little laying of letters together, he found the same to be this, "Remember Lot's wife." After which they concluded that it was the pillar of salt into which Lot's wife was turned. Which sudden and amazing sight gave them occasion for some profitable discourse.

I saw then that they went on their way to a pleasant river, even "the river of the water of life."

Now their way lay just upon the bank of this river; here they walked with great delight; they drank also of the water of the river, which was pleasant and enlivening to their weary spirits. Besides, on the banks, were green trees with all manner of fruit; and the leaves they ate healed diseases that are incident to those that heat their blood by travel. On either side of the river was also a meadow, curiously beautified with lilies; and it was green all the year long, and here they might lie down safely. When they awoke they gathered fruit of the trees, and drank again of the water of the river, and then lay down again to sleep. Thus they did several days and nights.

So when they were disposed to go on—for they were not as yet at their journey's end, they ate and drank and departed.

Now they had not journeyed far, when the river and the way for a time parted, at which they were sorry, yet they durst not go out of the way. The way from the river was rough, and their feet tender, so the pilgrims were discouraged. Wherefore, as they went on, they wished for a better way. Now, on the left hand of the road was a meadow, and a stile to go over into it, called By-path meadow. After some debate with themselves, and seeing that a path lay along by the way on the other side of the fence, Christian leading the way, they went over the stile, and found the road very easy to their feet.

Soon looking before them, they espied a man walking as they did, and his name was Vain-Confidence. So they asked him whither that way led. He said, To the Celestial gate. So they followed, and he went before them. But behold the night came on, and it grew very dark; so that they lost the sight of him that went before.

Now Vain-Confidence not seeing the way fell into a deep pit, which was on purpose to catch vain-glorious fools, and was dashed in pieces with his fall.

Christian and his fellow heard him fall. So they called, but there was none to answer, only they heard a groaning. And now it began to rain, and thunder, and lighten, in a most dreadful manner, and the water rose amain.

Then were Christian and Hopeful alarmed, and lamented that they had gone out of the right way. Still they adventured to go back; but it was so dark, and the flood was so high, that in their going back they had like to have been drowned.

Neither could they, get again to the stile that night. Wherefore at last, lighting under a little shelter, they sat down there till the day broke ; but being weary, they fell asleep.

Now there was not far from the place where they lay, a castle, called Doubting Castle, the owner whereof was Giant Despair, and it was in his grounds they now were sleeping ; wherefore he, getting up in the morning early, and walking up and down in his fields caught Christian and Hopeful asleep in his grounds.

Then with a grim and surly voice he bade them awake, and asked them whence they were, and what they did in his grounds. They told him they were pilgrims and that they had lost their way.

Then said the giant, "You have this night trespassed on me by trampling in and lying on my grounds, and therefore you must go along with me."

So they were forced to go, because he was stronger than they. They also had but little to say, for they knew themselves in a fault. The giant, therefore, drove them before him, and put them into his castle, into a very dark dungeon. Here, then, they lay from Wednesday morning till Saturday night without one bit of bread or drop of drink, or light, or any to ask how they did; they were, therefore, here in evil case, and were far from friends and acquaintance.

Now Giant Despair had a wife, named Diffidence: so when he was gone to bed he asked her what he had best do to them. She counselled him to beat them without mercy. So when he arose, he getteth him a grievous crab-tree cudgel, and goes down into the dungeon to them, and there first falls to rating of them as if they were dogs. Then he falls upon them, and beats them fearfully, so that they were not able to help themselves, or to turn them upon the floor. This done, he withdraws, and leaves them to their misery; so all that day they spent their time in nothing but sighs and bitter lamentations.

The next night, she, talking

again with her husband, and understanding that they were yet alive, did advise him to counsel them to make away with themselves. So in the morning he goes to them in a surly manner, and told them, that since they were never like to come out of that place, their only way would be forthwith to make an end to themselves, either with knife, halter, or poison; for why, said he, should you choose to live, see it is attended with so much bitterness?

But they desired him to let them go. With that he looked ugly upon them, and rushing to them, had doubtless made an end of them himself, but that he fell into one of his fits, for he sometimes in sunshiny weather fell into fits, and lost for a time the use of his hands: wherefore he withdrew, and left them as before to consider what to do. Then did the prisoners consult between themselves whether it was best to take his counsel or no.

Poor Christian felt completely crushed, but Hopeful comforted him. So they continued together in the dark that day, in a sad and doleful condition.

Well, towards evening the giant goes down again, to see if his prisoners had taken his counsel But when he came there he found them alive; and truly, alive was all; for now, for want of bread and water, and by reason of the wounds they received, they could do little but breathe. But I say, he found them alive; at which he fell into a grievous rage, and told them, that seeing they had disobeyed his counsel, it should be worse with them than if they had never been born.

At this they trembled greatly, and I think that Christian fell into a swoon; but coming a little to, they renewed their discourse about the giant's counsel, and whether yet they had best take it or no. Now Christian again seemed for doing it; but Hopeful made strongly against it.

Night being come again, and the giant and his wife in bed, she asked him of the prisoners: to which he replied, "They are sturdy rogues; they choose rather to bear all hardships than to make away with themselves."

Then said she, "Take them into the castle-yard to-morrow, and show them the bones and skulls of those that thou hast already killed and make them believe, ere a week comes to an end, thou wilt tear them in pieces, as thou hast done those."

So when the morning was come the giant did as his wife had bidden him, and said:—"And so within ten days I will do to you; get you down to your den again." And with that he beat them all the way thither.

PILGRIM'S PROGRESS. 143

Dungeon of Giant Despair.

They lay, therefore, all day on Saturday in a lamentable case, as before. Now, when night was come, Mrs. Diffidence and her husband began to renew their discourse of their prisoners; and the old giant wondered that he could neither by blows nor counsel bring them to an end. With that his wife replied, "I fear that they live in hopes that some will come to relieve them; or that they have picklocks about them by means of which they hope to escape."

"And sayest thou so, my dear?" said the giant; "I will therefore search them in the morning."

Well, on Saturday, about midnight, they began to pray, and

continued in prayer till almost break of day.

Now, a little before it was day, good Christian, as one half amazed broke out in this passionate speech:—

"What a fool am I, thus to lie in a noisome dungeon, when I may as well walk at liberty? I have a key in my bosom called Promise, that will, I am persuaded, open any lock in Doubting Castle."

Then said Hopeful, "That is good news; good brother, pluck it out of thy bosom, and try."

Then Christian pulled it out of his bosom, and began to try at the dungeon-door, whose bolt, as he turned the key, gave back, and the door flew open with ease, and Christian and Hopeful both came out. Then he went to the outward door that leads into the castle-yard, and with his key opened that door also. After that he went to the iron gate, for that must be opened too; but that lock went desperately hard, yet the key did open it.

Then they thrust open the gate to make their escape with speed; but that gate, as it opened, made such a creaking that it waked Giant Despair, who hastily rising to pursue them, felt his limbs to fail, for his fits took him again. Then they went on, and came to the King's highway, and so were safe.

Now, when they were gone over the stile, they began to contrive what they should do to prevent those that shall come after from falling into the hand of Giant Despair. So they erected there a pillar, and engraved upon the side thereof this sentence:

"Over this stile is the way to Doubting Castle, which is kept by Giant Despair, who despiseth the King of the Celestial country, and seeks to destroy his holy pilgrims." Many, therefore, that followed after, read what was written, and escaped the danger.

Then they went on till they came to the Delectable Mountains, which mountains belong to the Lord of that hill of which we have before spoken. So they went up to the mountains, to behold the gardens and orchards, the vineyards and fountains of water; where also they drank and washed themselves, and did freely eat of the vineyards.

Now there were on the tops of these mountains shepherds feeding their flocks, and they stood by the highway side. The pilgrims, therefore, went to them, and leaning upon their staffs, as is common with weary pilgrims when they stand to talk with any by the way, they asked.

"Whose Delectable mountains are these; and whose are the sheep that feed upon them?"

Shep. "These mountains are

Emmanuel's land, and they are within sight of his city; and the sheep are also his, and he laid down his life for them."

I saw also in my dream, that when the shepherds perceived that they were wayfaring men, they also put questions to them. And when the shepherds heard their answers, being pleased therewith, they looked very lovingly upon them, and said,

"Welcome to the Delectable Mountains."

The shepherds, whose names were Knowledge, Experience, Watchful, and Sincere, had them to their tents, and made them partake of what they had. They said moreover,

"We would that you should stay here a while to solace yourselves with the good of these Delectable Mountains."

Then they told them that they were content to stay. So they went to their rest that night, because it was very late.

Then I saw in my dream that in the morning the shepherds called up Christian and Hopeful to walk with them upon the mountains. So they went forth with them, and walked a while having a pleasant prospect on every side. Then said the shepherds one to another, "Shall we show these pilgrims some wonders?"

So when they had concluded to

do it, they led them first to the top of a hill called Error, which was very steep, and bid them look down to the bottom. So Christian and Hopeful looked down, and saw at the bottom several men dashed to pieces by a fall they had from the top.

Then said Christian, "What meaneth this?"

The shepherds answered, "Have you not heard of them that were made to err, by hearkening to Hymeneus and Philetus, concerning the faith of the resurrection of the body?"

They answered, "Yes."

Then said the shepherds, "Those that you see lie dashed in pieces unburied, at the bottom of this mountain are they, for an example to others."

Then I saw that they led them to the top of another mountain, named Caution, and bid them look afar off; which they did, and saw several men walking up and down among the tombs that were there; the men were blind, and stumbled sometimes upon the tombs.

Then said Christian, "What means this?"

The shepherds then answered, "Did you not see, a little below these mountains, a stile that led into a meadow, on the left hand of the way?"

They answered, "Yes."

Then said the shepherds, "From that stile there goes a path that leads directly to Doubting Castle, kept by Giant Despair; and these men wandering out of their way were taken by him and cast into his dungeon; at last he put out their eyes, and led them among those tombs, where he has left them to wander to this very day."

Then Christian and Hopeful looked upon one another, with tears gushing out, but yet said nothing to the shepherds.

Then the shepherds led them to another place, where was a door on the side of a hill; and they opened the door, and bid them look in. They looked in, and saw that within it was very dark and smoky; they also thought that they heard a rumbling noise as of fire, and a cry of some tormented, and that they smelt the scent of brimstone.

Then said Christian, "What means this?"

The shepherds told them, "This is a by-way to hell, a way that hypocrites go in at."

Then said the pilgrims one to the other, "We had need cry to to the Strong for strength."

Shep. "Aye, and you will have need to use it, when you have it, too."

By this time the pilgrims had a desire to go forward, and the shepherds a desire they should; so they walked together towards the end of the mountains. Then said the shepherds one to another,

"Let us here show the pilgrims the gates of the Celestial City, if they have skill to look through our perspective-glass."

The pilgrims lovingly accepted the motion: so they led them to the top of a high hill called Clear, and gave them the glass to look.

Then they tried to look; but the remembrance of that last thing that the shepherds had shown them made their hands shake, by means of which impediment they could not look steadily through the glass; yet they thought they saw something like the gate, and also some of the glory of the place.

When they were about to depart, one of the shepherds gave them a note of the way.

Another of them bid them beware of the Flatterer.

The third bid them take heed that they slept not upon the Enchanted Ground.

And the fourth bid them God speed. So I awoke from my dream.

And I slept and dreamed again, and saw the two pilgrims going down the mountains along the highway towards the city.

Now, a little below these mountains, on the left hand, lieth the country of Conceit; from which country there comes into the way in which the pilgrims walked, a little crooked lane. Here, therefore, they met with a very brisk lad, and his name was Ignorance.

So Christian asked him from what parts he came, and whither he was going.

"Sir, I was born in the country that lieth off there, and I am going to the Celestial City."

Chr. "But how do you think to get in at the gate, for you may find some difficulty there?"

"As other good people do," said he.

Christian asked him other questions tending to teach him of the way, but the replies of Ignorance showed him to be so wise in his own conceit, that, approaching Hopeful, Christian said to him in a whisper,

"There is more hope of a fool than of him."

So they determined to outgo him at present, hoping that he would reflect to his profit upon what had been suggested to him. Therefore they went on and Ignorance came after.

Now, they entered a very dark lane, where they met a man whom seven devils had bound with strong cords, and were carrying back to the door that they saw on the side of the hill. Then the pilgrims began to tremble; yet, Christian looked to see if he knew him; and he thought it might be one Turnaway, that dwelt in the town of Apostasy. But he did not perfectly see his face, for he hung his head like a thief that is found; but Hopeful looked after him, and espied on his back this inscription, "Wanton professor, and damnable apostate."

This sad sight caused Christian to remember, and then to tell Hopeful of what happened to a pilgrim hereabouts, whose name was Little-Faith of the town of Sincere. He was set upon and robbed in Dead-man's Lane, by three sturdy rogues, Faint-Heart, Mistrust, and Guilt. But they did not succeed in getting all he had, for hearing that Great-Grace, was a-coming, they fled, and did not get at his jewels. But poor Little-Faith was forced afterwards to beg to his journey's end. With his jewels he could not part, for had they been missing, there would be no entrance for him at the gate of the Celestial City.

Upon this experience of Little-Faith, the two loving pilgrims extracted lessons of profit as they journeyed on towards Mount Zion.

So they went on, and Ignorance followed, till they came to a place where they saw a way put itself into their way, and seemed as straight as the way which they should go; and here they knew not which of the two to take, and they stood still to consider. As they were thinking, behold a man black of flesh, but covered with a very light robe, came to them, and asked them why they stood.

They answered, they were going to the Celestial City, but knew not which of these ways to take.

"Follow me," said the man, "it is thither that I am going."

So they followed him in the way that but now came into the road, which by degrees turned, and turned them so far from the Celestial City, that in a little time their faces were turned away from it; yet they followed him. But by-and-by, before they were aware, he led them both within the compass of a net, in which they were both entangled; and with that the white robe fell off the black

Entangled in a net.

man's back. Then they saw where they were. Wherefore there they lay crying some time, for they could not get out.

Thus they lay bewailing themselves in the net; at last they espied a shining One coming towards them with a whip of small cords in his hand. He asked them whence they came, and what they did there. They told him that they were poor pilgrims going to Zion, but were led out of their way by a black man clothed in white.

Then said he with the whip, It is Flatterer, a false apostle, that hath transformed himself into an angel of light. So he rent the net, and let the men out. Then said he to them, Follow me, that I may set you in your way again.

So he led them back to the way which they had left to follow the Flatterer. Then after further questioning and reproving them, he commanded them to lie down; which when they did, he chastised them sore; and as he chastised them, he said, "As many as I love, I rebuke and chasten; be zealous, therefore, and repent."

This done, he bid them go on their way, and take good heed to their directions. So they thanked him for all his kindness, and went meekly along the right way.

Now, after a while they perceived afar off, one coming softly, and alone, all along the highway, to meet them, with his back towards Zion.

So he drew nearer and nearer, and at last came up to them. His name was Atheist, and he asked them whither they were going.

When Christian told him he fell into a very great laughter, and said there was no such place as Mount Zion, and that they were fools to seek further to find it.

So they turned away from the man; and he, laughing at them, went his way.

I then saw in my dream, that they went on until they came into a country whose air naturally tended to make one drowsy. Here Hopeful began to be very dull, and said to Christian, "I can scarcely hold open mine eyes; let us lie down here, and take one nap."

"By no means," said the other. Do you not remember that one of the shepherds bid us beware of the Enchanted Ground?"

Then Christian proposed, to prevent drowsiness, that they should engage in some good discourse. So he and Hopeful, after singing a hymn, held sweet communion a long time together; and Hopeful told Christian of all the Lord had done for his soul; and how he, the Crucified, had revealed Himself to him as the "chiefest among ten thousand," and the one "altogether lovely." And thus they passed along safely most of the Enchanted Ground, that dangerous portion of their travel heavenward.

I saw then in my dream, that Hopeful looking back, saw Ignorance, whom they had left behind, coming after.

"Look," said he to Christian, "how far yonder youngster loitereth behind! Let us tarry for him." So they did.

Then Christian said to him, "Come away, man; why do you stay so behind?"

Ignor. "I take my pleasure in walking alone, even more a great deal than in company, unless I like it the better."

"But however, come up, and let us talk away the time in this solitary place. Come, how do you do? How stands it between God and your soul now?"

Ignor. "I hope well; for I am always full of good motions, that come into my mind to comfort me as I walk."

Then Christian pressed Ignorance closely but kindly as to the nature of his hopes, and showed him how vain they were, but the conceited fellow wrangled with them and spoke reproachfully of what he knew not. At last he said to them:—

"You go so fast I cannot keep pace with you; do you go on before: I must stay a while behind."

So they went on apace before,

and Ignorance came hobbling after. Then said Christian to his companion,

"I much pity this poor man: I fear it will go ill with him at last."

After some further talk of the good use of the right kind of fear in a christian's experience, and also of some they knew who started on pilgrimage but did not adventure far, our brother pilgrims at last passed over the Enchanted Ground.

They were now come into the country of Beulah where the air was very sweet and pleasant; and the way lying directly through it they solaced themselves there for a season. Here they heard continually the singing of birds, and saw flowers bloom, and heard the turtle in the land. In this country the sun shineth night and day: wherefore this was beyond the valley of the Shadow of Death, and also out of the reach of giant Despair: neither could they from this place so much as see Doubting Castle.

Here they were within sight of the city they were going to; also here some of the inhabitants thereof met them; for in this land the shining ones commonly walked, because it was upon the borders of heaven.

Here they had no want of corn and wine; for in this place they met with abundance of what they had sought for in all their pilgrimage.

Now, as they walked in this land, they had much rejoicing; and drawing near to the city, they had yet a more perfect view thereof. It was builded of pearls and precious stones, also the streets thereof were paved with gold; so that Christian with desire fell sick; Hopeful also had a fit or two of the same disease.

But being a little strengthened, they walked on their way, and came yet nearer, where were orchards, vineyards, and gardens, whose gates opened to the highway. Now, as they came up to these places, the gardener said, "They are the King's and are planted here for his own delight, and also for the solace of pilgrims." So he bid them refresh themselves ; he also showed them there the King's walks and arbors and here they tarried and slept.

And when they awoke, they addressed themselves to go up to the city. But the city was so extremely glorious, that they could behold it, only through an instrument made for that purpose. So I saw, that as they went on, there met them two men in raiment that shone like gold, also their faces shone as the light.

Christian and his companion asked the men to go along with them. So they went on together till they came in sight of the gate.

Now betwixt them and the gate was a river; but there was no bridge to go over, and the river was very deep. At the sight of this river the pilgrims were much stunned; but the men that went with them said, "You must go through, or you cannot come to the gate."

The pilgrims, especially Christian, began to despond, and looked this way and that, but no way could be found by them by which they might escape the river.

Then they asked the men if the waters were all of a depth. They said, No; yet they could not help them in that case; for, said they, "you shall find it deeper or shallower as you believe in the King of the place."

They then drew near to the water, and entering, Christian began to sink, and crying out to his good friend Hopeful, he said,

"I sink in deep waters; the billows go over my head; all his waves go over me. Selah."

Then said the other,

"Be of good cheer, my brother: I feel the bottom, and it is good."

Then said Christian,

"Ah, my friend, the sorrows of death have compassed me about, I shall not see the land that flows with milk and honey."

And with that a great darkness and horror fell upon Christian, so

Crossing the River of Death.

that he could not see before him. All his words tended to discover that he had horror of mind and heart-fears that he should never obtain entrance in at the gate. Here also, some thoughts of the sins that he had committed both since and before he began to be a pilgrim, troubled him.

Hopeful therefore had much ado to keep his brother's head above water; he also endeavored to comfort him saying, "Brother I see the gate, and men standing by to receive us!"

But Christian would answer, "It is you, it is you they wait for; for you have been hopeful ever since I knew you."

Then Hopeful further kept him

up with words of golden promise, left by their Saviour-Prince gone on before them, to comfort pilgrims: then I saw in my dream that Christian was in a muse a while.

At last Christian broke out with a loud voice, "Oh, I see Him again; and he tells me, 'When thou passest through the waters, I will be with thee; and through the rivers, they shall not overflow thee.'"

Then they both took courage, and the enemy was after that as still as a stone, until they were gone over. Christian therefore presently found ground to stand upon. and so it followed that the rest of the river was but shallow.

Thus they got over.

Now, upon the bank of the river, on the other side, they saw the two shining men again, waiting for them, and with them, they went along towards the gate.

Now the pilgrims went up the hill with ease, because they had these two men to lead them; they likewise had left their mortal garments behind them in the river. They therefore went up with speed, through the air, sweetly talking as they went, being comforted because they had safely got over the river, and had such glorious ones to attend them. The talk also that they had with the shining ones was about the glory of the place to which they were going.

"There," said they, "is Mount Sion, the heavenly Jerusalem, the innumerable company of angels, and the spirits of just men made perfect. You are going now," said they, "to the paradise of God, wherein you shall see the tree of life, and eat of the never-fading fruits thereof: and when you come there you shall have white robes given you, and your walk and talk shall be every day with the King, even all the days of eternity. There you shall not see again such things as you saw when you were in the lower region upon the earth, to wit, sorrow, sickness, affliction, and death; 'for the former things are passed away.' You are going to Abraham, to Isaac, and Jacob, and to the prophets, men that God hath taken away from the evil to come, and that are now 'resting upon their beds, each one walking in his righteousness.'

The men then asked, "What must we do in the holy place?"

To whom it was answered,

"You must there receive the comfort of all your toil, and have joy for all your sorrow; you must reap what you have sown, even the fruit of all your prayers, and tears, and sufferings, for the King by the way. In that place you must wear crowns of gold, and enjoy the perpetual sight and vision of the Holy One; for there you shall see him as he is. There also you shall serve Him continually with praise, with shouting and thanksgiving, whom you desired to serve in the world, though with much difficulty, because of the infirmity of your flesh. There your eyes shall be delighted with seeing, and your ears with hearing the pleasant voice of the Mighty One. There you shall enjoy your friends again that are gone thither before you; and there you shall with joy receive even every one that follows into the holy place after you. There also you shall be clothed with glory and majesty, and be put into an equipage fit to ride out with the King of glory. When he shall come with sound of trumpet in the clouds, as upon the wings of the wind, you shall come with him; and when he shall sit upon the throne of judgment, you shall sit by him; yea, and when he shall pass sentence upon all the workers of iniquity, let them be angels or men, you also shall have a voice in that judgment, because they were his and your enemies. Also, when he shall again return to the city, you shall go too with sound of trumpet, and be ever with him.

While they were thus drawing towards the gate, behold a company of the heavenly host came out to meet them: and they bade them welcome.

There came out also several of

the King's trumpeters, clothed in white and shining raiment. These trumpeters saluted Christian and his fellow with ten thousand welcomes; and this they did with shout and sound of trumpet.

This done, they compassed them round on every side; as it were to guard them through the upper regions, continually sounding as they went, with melodious noise, in notes on high; so that the very sight was, as if heaven itself had come down to meet them. And now were these two men, as it were, in heaven, before they came to it, being swallowed up with the sight of angels, and with hearing of their melodious notes. Here also they had the city itself in view; and they thought they heard all the bells therein to ring, to welcome them. Thus they came up to the gate.

Now when they were come up to the gate, there was written over it, in letters of gold,

"BLESSED ARE THEY THAT DO HIS COMMANDMENTS, THAT THEY MAY HAVE RIGHT TO THE TREE OF LIFE, AND MAY ENTER IN THROUGH THE GATES INTO THE CITY."

Then I saw in my dream, that the shining ones bid them call at the gate: which they did. Then the pilgrims gave in unto those who looked over the gate the certificates, they had received in the beginning: these were carried in to the King, who, when he had read them, said, Where are the men? To whom it was answered, "They are standing without." The King then commanded to open the gate.

Now I saw in my dream, that these two men went in at the gate; and lo, as they entered, they were transfigured; and they had raiment put on that shone like gold. There were also some that met them with harps and crowns, and gave them to them. Then I heard in my dream, that all the bells in the city rang again for joy, and that it was said unto ihem, "ENTER YE INTO THE JOY OF YOUR LORD." I also heard the men themselves, that they sang with a loud voice, saying, "Blessing, and honour, and glory, and power, be unto Him that sitteth upon the throne, and unto the Lamb, for ever and ever."

Now, just as the gates were opened to let in the men, I looked in after them: and behold, the city shone like the sun; the streets also were paved with gold; and in them walked many men, with crowns on their heads, palms in their hands, and golden harps, to sing praises withal.

There were also some of them that had wings, and they answered one another without intermission, saying, Holy, holy, holy is the Lord. And after that they shut up the gates; which when I had seen, I wished myself among them.

Now, while I was gazing upon all these things, I turned my head to look back, and saw Ignorance come up to the river side; but he soon got over, and that with little difficulty. For there was then in that place one Vain-Hope, a ferryman, that with his boat helped him over; so he, as the others I saw, did ascend the hill, to come up to the gate; only he came alone.

When he was come up to the gate, he looked up to the writing that was above, and then began to knock, supposing that entrance should have been quickly administered to him; but he was asked by the men that looked over the top of the gate, "Whence come you? and what would you have?"

He answered, "I have ate and drunk in the presence of the King, and he has taught in our streets."

Then they asked him for his certificate, that they might go in and show it to the King: so he fumbled in his bosom for one, and found none. Then said they, "Have you none?" but the man answered not a word.

So they told the King, but he would not come down to see him, but commanded the two shining ones that conducted Christian and Hopeful to the city, to go out and take Ignorance, and bind him hand and foot, and lead him away. Then they took him up and carried him through the air to the door I saw in the side of the hill, and put him in there. Then I saw that there was a way to hell even from the gate of heaven, as well as from the city of Destruction.

So I awoke and behold, it was a dream.

END OF PART FIRST.

www.ingramcontent.com/pod-product-compliance
Lightning Source LLC
Chambersburg PA
CBHW032142160426
43197CB00008B/747